C000119028

Words
& Pictures

Linda Robinson

David Tarn

photography with a pen
poetry with a camera

Linda Robinson
& David Tarn

Published by
Scene as Seen Publishing

www.davidtarn.com

Designed & Produced by
Jeremy Mills Publishing Limited

www.jeremymillspublishing.co.uk

First Edition 2010
Text and images © Linda Robinson & David Tarn

ISBN 978-1-906600-52-5

All rights reserved. No part of this book may be
reproduced in any form or by any means without
prior permission in writing from the publisher.

Words & Pictures

photography with a pen
poetry with a camera

Linda Robinson
& David Tarn

Ironing

I hate ironing.

It steals my time
and robs joy from my day.

It makes me sweat and stoop
as I try to wrestle it into submission
on my battle-scarred ironing board.

It breeds overnight in my laundry basket
like over-sexed rabbits.
Multiplying.

Where is Mary Poppins when you need her?

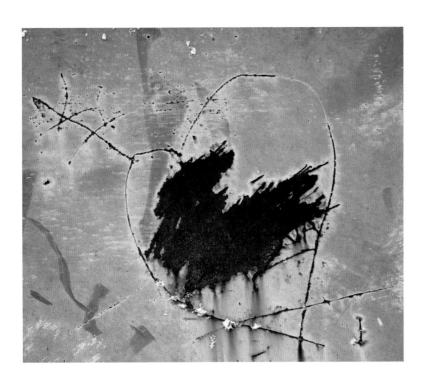

Lisa B loves Ian R 2006

She loved him. So much.
Since that first English class
when they'd shared a
text book.

The way his hair
curled out on one
side of his head.
That freckle under
his left eye.
His supermarket aftershave.
She loved everything about him.

Sitting at the same table
in the school dining hall.
Well, it wasn't
a coincidence, was it?
He must have planned it.
He wanted to be near her.
That was clear.
And soon he'd ask her out.
It was obvious.

She went to the
school dance.
Dark hair straightened.
Eyeliner caked
round watery blue eyes,
eager to share passionate
gazes with The Boy.
She waited and she
waited but he didn't show up.
'He got side-tracked on
the way' his best-friend said.

She counted her Maltesers out
into her lap on the bus home.
'He loves me, he loves me not',
passing The Boy outside a
corner shop,
Its neon glow illuminating
the curly blonde head he was kissing.
And her heart sank as she was
crushed by a crush.

Hiding Place

The smell of damp wood
mingles with tobacco smoke,
as crossword puzzles are filled in
during the cricket commentary
on that crackly old radio.

Then at dusk, he struggles with
the rusty old padlock,
snapping shut the door to
his private kingdom at the
bottom of the garden.

It's A Sign

No parking on
market days.
Wednesdays,
between 6.00am and 6.00pm.
Even though the market's
long gone,
packed away by three,
and all that remains in
empty parking bays are
mouldy oranges and
bits of broccoli.

Don't dare park there
because we're watching you.
Remember that.
We're watching YOU.

Don't forget to smile
at the CCTV vultures that
sit up on high,
craning their necks and
whirring into position
to get you into focus,
communicating with their
talking lamppost cousins.

Following you, stalking you,
all the way home.
Zooming in and peering through that gap in
your bedroom curtains at your
reflection in your wardrobe mirror.
Surveillance pornography.

You shouldn't mind if you
have nothing to hide
is the politician's credo.
But I do mind.

It's a sign.

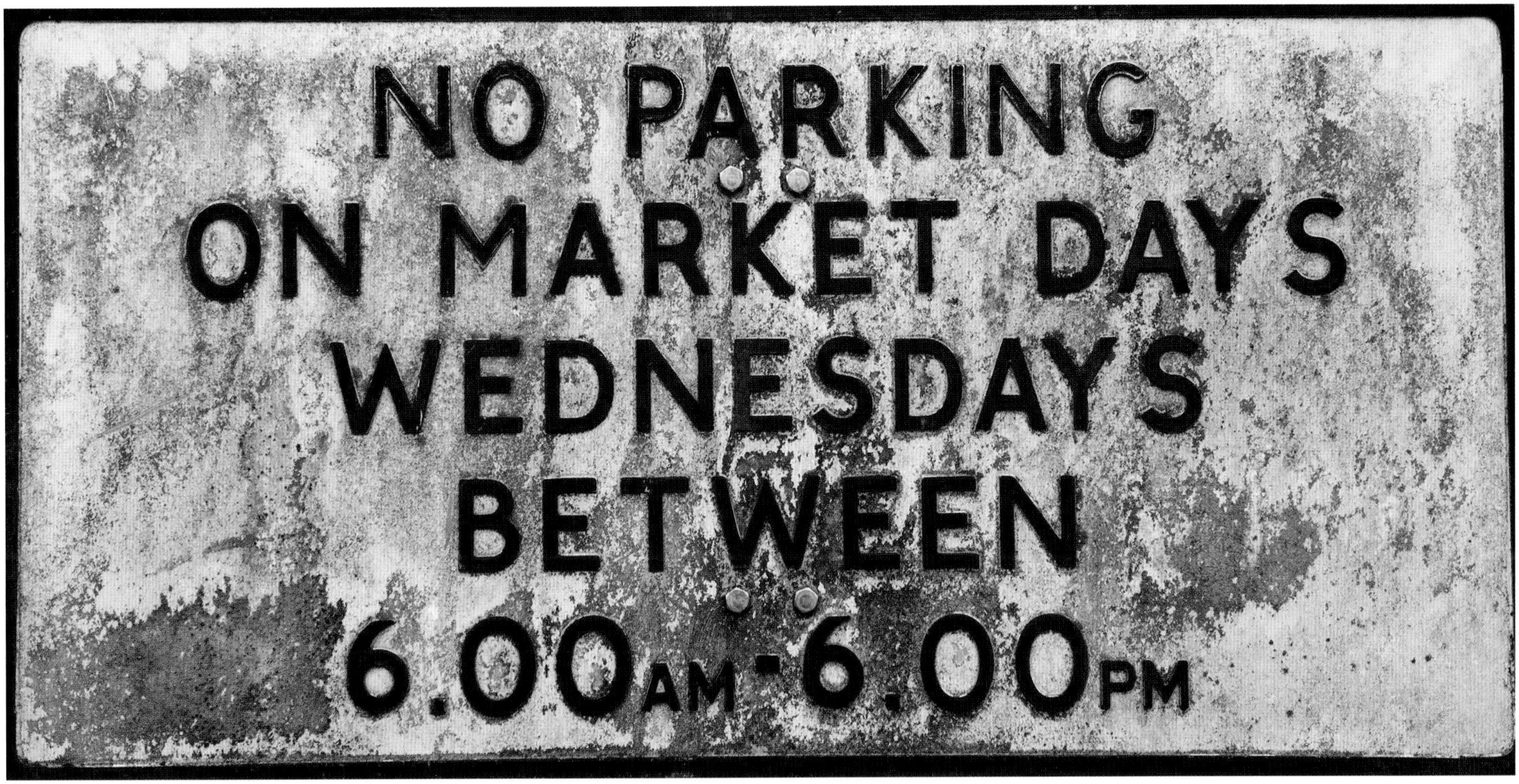
NO PARKING
ON MARKET DAYS
WEDNESDAYS
BETWEEN
6.00AM-6.00PM

Bitter/Sweet Romance

It was a place of urban decay,
its chipped and faded beauty
a poor man's Venice,
but it was ours.

Under leaden skies
we'd shelter in my car,
each moment stolen
from the rest of the world.

Her Cointreau smiles
lit up my life
over dinner by the river
in that discreet bistro.

Until real life stole her back,
and all I have left
is the taste of oranges.

When Love Departs

Love departs and humans shrink
in spirit and in stature.
aching for someone to touch them,
to hold them tightly,
to remind them that they are still alive.

Love departs and every fibre and nerve
of our being craves comfort.
The rock that is in our chest
makes breathing heavy,
until someone can roll away the stone.

Where is God?

I heard the radio report.
Another high school massacre.
The church counsellor offered
words of comfort to the numb,
grieving parents as a
commentator asked,
'How could this happen?
Where is God?'

The counsellor's reply
was tempered with the tone
of 'I told you so'.
'You drove Him out of your hearts,
your homes, your workplaces and
your schools, so how could
He be here today?'

Raging Whisper

I spoke with you for the last time yesterday.
It wasn't your voice any more.
That has already been stolen and awaits you
on the other side.
The raging whisper that is left is being
suffocated by your morphine.
Word by word until you are gone.

Locked In

She's locked in.
In her place.
Her eyes are small windows
offering fleeting glances to the
outside world she rejects.

Surrounded by life that's
frenetic and full of unpredictability.
Light and colour and sound
bombarding her senses.

She picks petals off flowers, again,
and smiles and smiles.
The edges of her lips
stretch as if to touch her earlobes.

Her rituals encircle her family,
drawing them into her existence.

They're locked in.

Can someone find the key?

Lonely Cloud

Where have you been today?
What did you see?
If only you could speak.
I wish I could lasso you
and pull you down to earth
so that I could lie on you
and sink into your marshmallow-like
folds for the perfect sleep.

A – Z

Take our hopes and dreams
for you in your backpack
as you trundle around the
world in your unwashed clothes.
The sand between your toes
a small irritation as you camp on
exotic beaches with strangers.

Take your hopes and dreams
for us in your heart
as you Skype home daily,
checking that we are okay and
functioning without you.
Can we manage without your
loving chaos and energy?

Take life in your stride
as change makes you feel
scared and life's road map
is sometimes spoilt by that
big staple in the middle.
Just follow the A – Z from birth
to big sky as best you can.

Suntan

She smoothes her towel on the sand,
lifts it up once more to remove a pebble,
then smoothes it again across
the white sand of her grey day dreams.

Once seated, she ceremoniously
decants her sun milks and oils,
drenching her rounded belly with the potions
until her skin's thirst is assuaged.

Years of sun worshipping,
her skin would make a fine handbag,
its texture and hue next season's fashion.

She lies back,
fingers outstretched like Spanish fans.
Closed eyes watching orange spangles
until she fries at noon.

Oh, Coco!
What did you start?
A fashionable hedonism that
cultivates fatal flaws.

Sea

Do you think I don't know
you and your secrets?
I know everything.
I listen to your every thought,
every whisper, every heartbeat.
Happy or sad
I know you too well.
But I will never tell
your secrets.
They are safe with me.
I will take them away with me,
wash them in my waves
and store them on the wind.
Out of sight.
Out of mind.

White Horses

They creep up on the wind,
slowly building pace and force.
Walk, trot, canter.
Then into a roaring gallop.
Thundering in towards the breakwater.
No refusal at the worn stone hurdle as
they smash violently into its structure.
Impact. Aqueous explosion.
Crashing white plumes of
salty foaming chaos.

Then stillness.

Sun glints off their hoof prints
on slowly calming water.
Imaginary horseshoes left behind by
those beautiful white horses.

Grasslands

Tall grasses bow and sway,
the wind caressing each
stalk and strand.
Slowly then quickly,
teasing and chasing from
root to tip in
Nature's dance.
Sensuously shifting
in descending mists,
their silhouettes like
wedding day lace.

Ashes to Ashes

Amongst dancing grasses
and whispering leaves,
I choose today to share you
with the earth.
Where we made memories
and promises,
I leave you one last time,
to witness crimson sunsets
scented by wild flowers
on the evening breeze,
until one day I will join you.

November Day

Today I thought of you.
I remembered you at
11 o'clock on the 11th day of the 11th month.
You filled my thoughts.

I picked up a newspaper in a shop
as the radio high on a shelf
asked for two minutes silence
in memory of people like you.

I never knew you,
but I knew you had a shrapnel scar
that my father could put his child-size
fist through in your weary shoulder.

And now our silence and poppies
are all that we have left to
remember you.
A paltry gift for your sacrifice.

HODGSON.THOMAS
HODGSON.ROBERT
HOEY.JAMES P.
HOGAN.W.
HOGARTH.JAMES S.
HOLMES.WILLIAM
HOLMES.SAMUEL
HOPE.JOHN J. M.M.
HOPPER.ROBERT E.
HORSLEY.J.W.
HORSLEY.J.E.
HORSPOLE.JOHN WM
HOUSTON.WM S.
HUDSON.THOMAS
HUNTER.JOHN ED
JACKSON.HENRY
JAMES.DAVID WM
JELLY.CHRIS JAS
JENKINSON.HERBT
JENNINGS.MATTHEW
JONES.JOHN.

LOWTHER.JOS.H.
LUPTON.STEPHEN.G.
LYNCH.FRANCIS
LYNCH.FRANK W.
LYNCH.HENRY
LYTH.HARRY
McCARTHY.JAMES
McCLELLAND.GEO.
McCLELLAND.OSWD
McDONALD.EDWARD
McDONNELL.MICHL
McGREGOR.J.A.
McGREGOR.W.
McINTOSH.JAMES
McLAUGHLIN.JAS.T.
McMAHON.JOHN
McNALLY.JOHN J
MALABAR.JOHN.T.
MALONEY.JAMES
MARINE.WILLIAM
MARLEY.J.B.
MARTIN.WILLIAM E.

The Troubles

Peace.
That's what they want.
Well, some of them.

Others see an industry
of terror in decline.
What will they do
when they have no
more bombs to prime?

Look inside themselves
discovering that deep down
we all bleed the same.

Search

Search my sadness until
you find the cause.
Break it into tiny pieces
and throw it to the wind.

Search my soul until
you find its core.
Embrace it, cherish it,
lest it might fade away.

Search no longer for
I will not leave you.
Your good heart has
snared me forever.

Anger

You are like an uninvited guest
in my house
that breaks in,
pulls everything out of the cupboards,
then leaves my life in chaos.

I chase after you sometimes
in the belief
that if I capture you,
I can control you
and you will be at my command.

But you are too slippery for that.
You like to expose me.
Show my true passion.
Reveal my flaws
for everyone to witness and to judge.

Whether The Weather Will Come? – Summer 1998

We've not had a summer yet.
Not in the North.
So you smug Southerners
deserve your smog and your blocked
roads to ferryports.

I have no sympathy
as I perform my yoga postures
in front of my T.V.,
the weatherman telling me I
have more rainy days ahead
while you are basking on pebbled beaches.

He says that you'll have another sizzling salad day,
while I turn up my central heating
and cook another gravy dinner.

A Poverty Wind

It comes up sometimes
when you least expect it.
The days of bounty disappear in
the bottom of a chipped pint glass,
as you watch the malty foam
slowly sliding down the clear sides.
No big catch today, just sprats.
Fortune comes and goes but when
the poverty wind comes,
hold your breath and pray.

30 St. Mary Axe

Gherkin.
You're not to everyone's taste.
You and yours leave us in
a financial pickle.
Piquant but unpalatable,
a feast for the eye
on the City skyline.
A gleaming phallus that
helped shaft the world.

The Lost Shoppers

As colourful as the Sistine Chapel,
they are our new places of worship.
Neon lit, they lure us with their
free parking and under-cover malls
to part with our money.

SALE TODAY!
An invitation to buy more things
we don't need or don't fit,
but they're too cheap to miss,
aren't they, with their final
75% off.

They spray us with perfume
and give us free makeovers,
tell us how we look so much
better in that cashmere sweater.
How can we resist?

Taking the shopping bags
out of the car boot and into
our homes, the pangs of guilt
arrive before the credit card
bill hits the doormat.

And down the road Mrs. Brown
picks out the clothes from her new
wardrobe, cuts off the labels,
and prepares to be the best-dressed
bankrupt the court has ever seen.

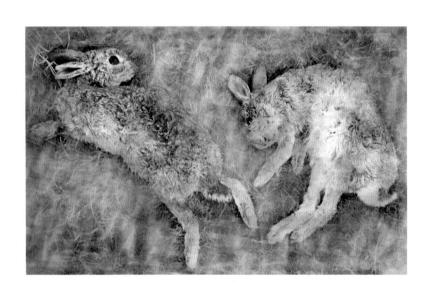

Country Life

They come every weekend,
breaking the sleepy rhythms
of the villages with their
growling Chelsea tractors.

Lucinda and Milo play
in the neatly kept garden
while Mummy pours Pimms
on the newly paved patio.

As birdsong diminishes
and the inky black night
of the country descends,
Daddy drives five miles
to pick up the signal
on his Blackberry,
returning when his children
are tucked up in bed.

As the cockerel heralds
another day's beginning,
they yawn and stretch their
city muscles before
returning to sleep.

Nearby, a pig farmer
finishes his third
whisky of the day and
throws red letters on
the fire-back.

Seasons

Summer leaves me with sad eyes,
its kaleidoscope of dancing colours
fade and fall
as time parades another season change
through life's revolving door.

Faster and harder,
hotter and colder.
Turning and turning until
time and seasons become a blur,
spinning beyond our control.

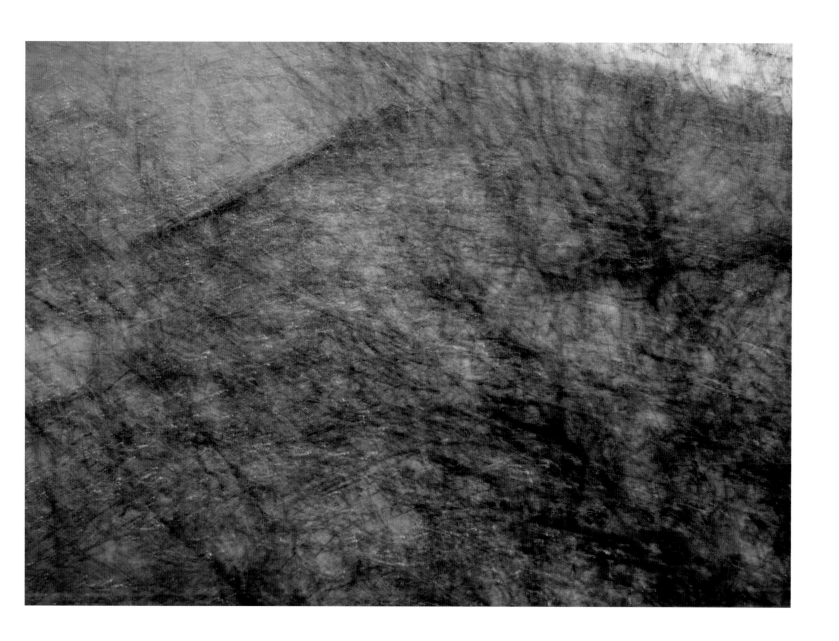

Meadow Flowers

Easel, paper and paint
implore me to capture you,
your dancing heads of
pink and blue and white and red.
To chase you, to stay ahead of you,
to know your every petal as
you dry on my page
in the dying day's sun.
Your perfection frozen in time
before you decay and fall
back to the earth.

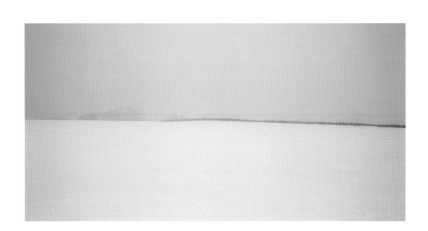

Winter Trees

Winter trees silhouetted against
early morning mists,
their black lace-like branches
Mother Nature's mantillas.
They sway proudly
in the breeze.
Every day is Sunday best.

Hunting Baby Rainbows

Every slippery step took me closer
to the baby rainbows that
lived in the crashing water
that smoothed the ancient stones below
into giant tumbled gems of the Gods.

Water's Edge

Reeds like angel hair
bend in the breeze.
Squint into the light
and they become the aurora
borealis of the lake or
Nature's own fibre-optic lamp.

Buttertubs

Shadows from clouds
charge across your contours.
Cumulonimbus bullies chasing
cirrus stratus all the way home.

Your fells and dales rise and fall,
undulating like nature's giant water bed.
Purples, golds and rusts,
the texture of breadcrumbed suede.

Climbing your summits,
a labour of love
that makes the heart beat faster,
the lungs gasp for air
and the mind reel at your
majestic beauty.

How Big Is The Sky?

'How big is the sky?'
the little boy asked
as he took his crayons
to capture the scene.
'It's as big as my love
for you' his
father answered.
'Is that gigantic or
humongous?'
the little boy asked.
His father shook his head.
'Neither. It goes on forever.'

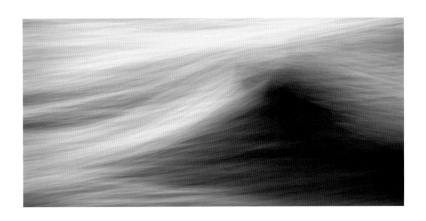

I am a wave

I am a wave.
Grey, turbulent, cold.
Lemming-like in my
pursuit of the horizon
that can never by reached.
My cross-current
over-arching with others
until you seek me out.
Your moon-like pull
controlling me completely.

On The Beach – 2046

Tattooed grandmothers
chase little girls playfully
along the water's edge.
The view out to the wind turbine rafts
looks almost as spectacular as
the large windmills in their back yards at home.
They revel in their global warming now that the
local drugstore sells a cure for everything,
but still worry about their world drowning
because the last man alive told them it
might happen tomorrow.

Missing You

Each sunrise and sunset
commemorates your absence.
The sea swells, breathes in,
then breathes out,
spilling onto the shore.
Its ebbs and flows
mesmerising me with its
promise of your return.
The sun and moon
change places over and over
as the calendar runs
out of months.
Your leaving is like a
million tiny deaths,
your return like a shower
of falling stars.

Stockholm Syndrome in the UK

Moulded like sugar paste
on his cheating mother's
'Happy Divorce' cake,
he knew the price of everything
but the value of nothing.

He graduated from her
'puppet academy'
the day he saw his father
as the ultimate cash cow
to be milked to death.

And he milked
and he milked
until his father
was wrung out
emotionally and financially,
making his mother very proud.

The 'poster boy' for
broken homes
stretched love to the limit
until its elastic strained,
frayed, then snapped.
Now difficult to repair,
never strong enough
to trust ever again.

Leaving

The road was melting
the day I left him,
closing the door on the
smell of freshly baked bread
I'd baked for his supper.

Walking through the meadow
I was calm,
as if being drawn serenely by
an angel's silken thread
into the unknown.

Then, as the sun began to set,
I sat and waited for you
on warm sandstone,
wondering what you would
look like.
Aroused with expectation.

Flaunt Yourself

Forget the boob jobs,
the face lifts and the tummy tucks.
Forget the face creams, the laser
treatments and the diets.
Forget the circuit training and
the jogging on the treadmill.
Stop chasing your youth and
embrace your age and experience.

Wrinkles are the barcodes of life.
Flaunt them.
You're not past your sell-by date yet.

Day-trippers

Some arrive in their little
strappy tops, white trousers
and fashion sandals,
on-trend sunglasses and
St. Tropez tans to climb Helvellyn.

More concerned about
breaking nails than necks,
they look great on the evening
news as the mountain rescue
teams stretcher them down.

The 'compass brigade's' expensive
kagoules rustle loudly as they
push their way to the front to see
another ill-prepared 'statistic' being rescued,
their plastic-bound maps
swinging down round their necks,
a professional rambler's pendulum.

As the latest 'statistic' is slid into
the back of a waiting ambulance,
they lean smugly on their walking
poles and break open another bar
of Kendal Mint Cake.

Path

You can follow me.
I'll show you the way.
Forget your last disappointing
visit to the spiritual supermarket,
its 'pick and mix' of faiths
that left you feeling sick.
The prayers, the incense,
the chanting, the fasting.
All will be fading memories
if you follow me because
I'm the next big thing.
All the celebrities think so.

Transporter Bridge

She towers above the river
in her blue working clothes.
Robust magnificence
from an age of industrial glory.
The Queen of the Tees flanked
by her concrete courtiers.

But at night she flaunts herself,
her beautiful bone structure lit
up for all to see.
Coquettish in her finery as she
sees off neon upstarts on the horizon.

Angel of the North

You stand aloft,
the colour of autumn,
resembling a Harryhausen creation,
your wings trembling in crosswinds.

One day you'll tear your feet out
of your concrete tomb
and stampede across nearby roads,
breaking free from captivity.

Retiring to a theme park
amongst fibre glass mountains,
giants and King Kong rides.
No longer alone.

Steel River

We are the children of the Steel River.
Our spirit forged on the anvil
of the Ironmasters ambition.

In the shadows of
the chimneys and the furnaces
we are indomitable and fierce,
yet open and loyal.
When our industrial
masters eat us up and
spit us out,
their pockets lined
like the last blast furnace,
we are dignified and proud.
Steel in our hearts and
steel in our spines.

From father to son
and father to son,
the baton of our industrial
heritage is handed on,
with many a false start in
the race to remain
relevant, economical, viable.

We will always be the children of the
Steel River
and if the sounds of industry are
one day stilled you will still hear us
roar.

Launch Yourself

Today you are on the launch pad
of tomorrow's dreams.
You are in the driving seat of a fast
car into the future.
Behind the controls of a beautiful
ship as she disappears from view,
crossing the horizon of contentment
to a land buzzing with new opportunities.
Go on. Take a leap of faith.
Start your own personal countdown and
launch yourself.

Love Through Time

When the world
spins to an end
and we embrace each
other one last time,
I will hold your gaze
and you will be
mine forever.

Into the darkness
or into the light,
we do not know
what lies ahead.
We only have the
truth and certainty
of each other.

Souls intertwined,
knitted together
with the fabric of
our lives,
we will go on
'til the last star
fades away.

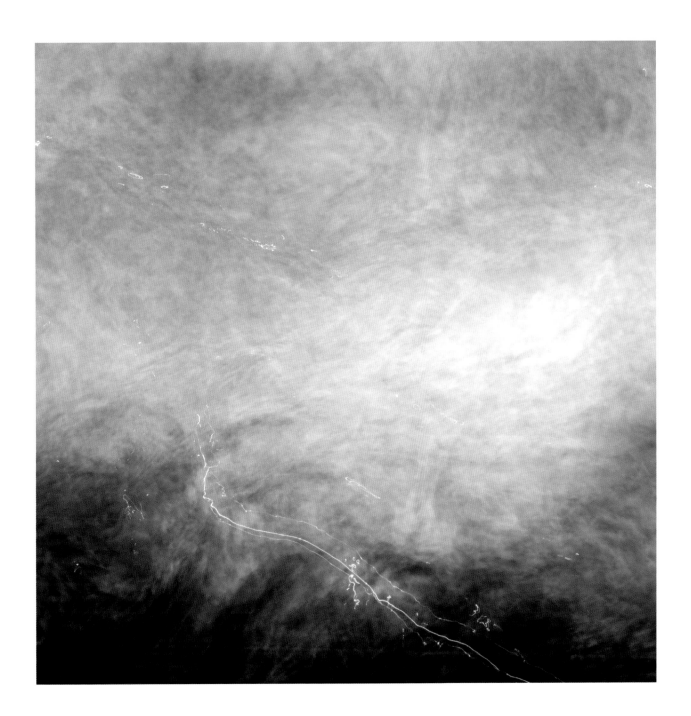

Saltwick Bay

Black Nab, lurking,
submarine-like and stealthy.
Waiting for Fate's hand to
lure its victims through
foaming seas to its
altar of destruction.
Its accomplices, those
biting easterlies,
relish their collusion
in this deception.
A shivering wreck
lies vulnerable and uncovered,
its souls once saved by selfless
gallantry that wiped the
smile off the Devil's face.

Still Standing

The landscape barren
around me.
I am alone.

Dry as an
elephant's hide.
Parched, unloved,
misunderstood.
Masquerading as someone
you think you know.

How can I grow, flourish,
prosper here?
Why would I bother?
Why would you care?

Do you understand me?
Do I understand myself?
Those words that come out
of my mouth are not mine
all of the time.
Sometimes they are said
to please you, anger you,
confuse you.

Even though my boughs are
stiff and unyielding,
my roots are supple.
They're your roots too.
We are still connected
you and I.
We still share the same
sunrises and sunsets,
only from different perspectives.

The Trip

His heart got bigger
and louder as the minibus
approached the farmhouse.
It leapt from his little chest,
tore through the minibus roof
and soared up into the big, blue sky
when he saw his first horse
in the field beside the barn.
As his spirit exploded into
a million coloured pieces through
his inner city pores,
the moment branded itself on his
sink-estate memory forever,
to entertain and tantalise between
visits to the local crack house.

A Perfect Moment

He watched the rain
from his desk beside
the window in his
suffocating office.
As the clock slowly
ticked and tocked its
way through more of his
squandered life,
he looked at his wristwatch.

Outside a streetlight spluttered
from red to dirty orange.
He slid his suit jacket
from the chairback,
switched off his Master
with the crisp click of a mouse
and made his way out of the
building that was his prison.

He walked head down
along the cobbled street,
rivulets of rain snaking down
between his frowning brows.
As he stepped off the kerb
into the rush hour traffic,
for one beautiful moment
he noticed the shining cobbles,
glistening like the perfect union
between molasses and Indian ink.
It took his breath away –
and it would never return.

Togetherness

My spirit travels across
the miles and skies.
My imagination soars
on the wind that brings
me to this seat.

Its blond wood guides
me to this place and
invites me to rest a while,
Cradling me like a
straight-backed parent,
protecting me as I relax,
let go of my senses
and drink in the
wonders of the lake.

From the first people to
new adventurers,
they've discovered the
world is perfect here.
Memories left behind
by previous spirits
hang heavy in the air,
then fall as raindrops
on the thirsty earth and
fill the lake with sacred
knowledge from above.

And we sit, still,
in body or in spirit,
together by the lake.

The Infant Stirs Once More

"This remarkable place, the youngest child of
England's enterprise, is an infant, but if an infant,
an infant Hercules" - W. E. Gladstone, visiting
Middlesbrough in 1862.

In those ironstone mines
carved from primitive beauty,
the first breath was taken,
the first muscle flexed.
From rural cradle
to industrial ancestral home,
the infant Hercules
grew with awesome power
and strength to build the world.

As the tides ebbed and flowed,
the infant became a rebellious teenager,
spreading out and challenging the world
to go faster, go further, go higher.
Precious skills honed through generations,
in the steelworks, the mines,
the shipyards and chemical plants.

All the while the Tees
bore witness to its favourite child
going out into the world,
leaving its shining signature on bridges,
railways, buildings and more.
A gleaming testimony to craft,
to dedication, to innovation.

And the infant's future children,
those black-eyed men,
their overalls and baitbags
reeking with the smell of the works,
came home with their fingers cracked
and bleeding from the hard frost of nightshifts,
never knowing their lungs were
storing up deadly surprises.

But they wouldn't change a minute
of those days on the tools,
The camaraderie, the craftsmanship,
the pride in making, building, showing
the world that they could make the best
and could make it for them too.

For those men, and now women, carry pride
in their hearts for their industrial heritage.
They don't always look back.
They look forward to shaping the world again.
The infant's memory is roused and
ready to flex its muscles once more.
To deliver what the future needs.

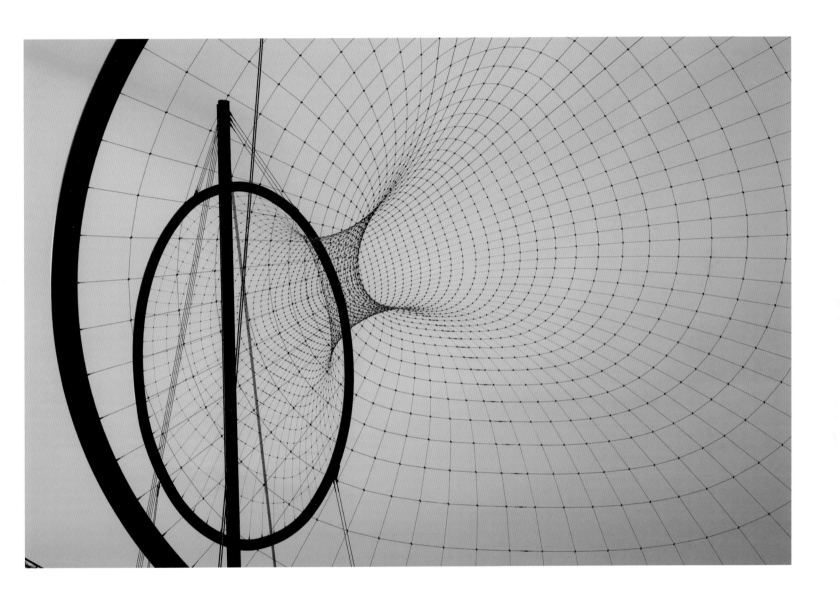

Photographers notes

I used to say that I was a landscape photographer, and for a while that was true. In all honesty though I have never felt truly comfortable with the title or description "photographer". Photography is for me, and always has been, a medium. I have never been enamoured of the process of photography. Never loved a camera or been excited by technique. When I was a "landscape photographer" my real passion was for the landscape, not the photography. The photography was an excuse to be out there in the landscape, seeing the contours of the land under all weather conditions and in all light at all times of the year. Out in the landscape I found beauty and peace.

These days it might appear as if my palate has expanded well beyond that which might traditionally be considered the landscape. Truth is though my subject remains beauty and peace, the difference these days is the number of places I can find those things. My philosophy of photography is that it is about the subject. It is not about the techniques used or the camera. It is not about the composition it's not even about the light. The best photographs are snap shots, that is photographs where the only motive for taking them was the subject.

The images in this book have that one thing in common, they were all without exception motivated by nothing other than the subject of the photograph. The techniques used vary, the equipment used varies, some were taken with very simple very high quality large format camera and lenses, some with the smallest of digital compact cameras and some with professional level digital slr cameras and lenses. Some of the images use a photograph as a starting point and the rest is "created" within the computer, a piece of digital art. My only motive for creating any of these images was the subject.

It has been a real pleasure collaborating with Linda Robinson and seeing words set to my pictures. Sometimes this has proven that while my motive for a photograph was entirely the subject, and while my technique has been flawless, and I have captured exactly that which I sought to capture, Linda's eye and Linda's words have revealed an altogether different subject for my photographs than the one I intended. When I took my photograph "No Parking" my subject was the sleepy rhythms of a market town and the wonderful texture provided by the years. I had no inkling of a creeping totalitarian state as suggested by Linda's poem "It's a sign". I then saw two policemen through the rain streaked and steamed windows of a coffee shop, and I saw a beauty and calm in the colours and shapes.

The subject of any of my photographs, while entirely the motive for taking the photograph, and while totally contained within the photograph might be less than obvious. That which was my subject might not be the subject you see. You will have your own narrative, your own point of view, and your own life experience to bring to the table. Likewise Linda's poem might bring to mind an entirely different image than the one presented here. I hope this book will be like a piece of ambient music, looking at its pages will clear the mind. I hope you will find beauty in all of the images, and that finding this beauty in images where none was expected you will then be able to find beauty in places you would not have thought to look.

For those who are interested in the technicalities, the camera used, the lens and the settings, the locations and dates of the photographs, as much as I know or can recall is presented alongside thumbnail views of the images in the next few pages.

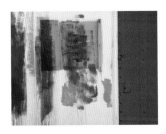

Title page: After Rothco
Canon G9 – 210mm lens
1/30th f4.8 50 ISO handheld
Builders hut Greenwich
17 July 2008

Ironing: Lady in Lavender
Casio XP700 – 180mm lens
Slow? F9.2 80 ISO handheld
Oxford Street London.
Deliberate camera movement
21st April 2006

Lisa B loves Ian R 2006: Pathos
Canon G9 – 210mm lens
1/60th f4.8 80 ISO handheld
Graffiti Middlesbrough
19th August 2008

Hiding place: Tin shed (support image)
Canon 5D – 35mm lens
0.4 seconds f22 50 ISO tripod
North Yorkshire Moors
23rd January 2007

Hiding place: The office (main image)
Canon 5D – 200mm lens
1.3 seconds f14 50 ISO tripod
Pickering North Yorkshire
27th November 2007

It's a sign: Police (support image)
Canon G9 –210mm lens
1/30th f4.8 80 ISO handheld
Newcastle upon Tyne
28th November 2009

It' a sign: No Parking (main image)
Canon 5D- 180mm lens
1/25th f8 50 ISO tripod
Sedburgh North Yorkshire
31st July 2008

Bitter/Sweet Romance: Gas
Canon 5D-45mm lens
1/60th f4 50 IOS handheld
Perspective corrected
postproduction
Gasometer Stockton on Tees
15th February 2008

When Love Departs: Stones on the shore
Canon 5D- 22mm lens
3.2 seconds f22 50 ISO tripod
Dunstanburgh
Northumberland
20th February 2009

Where is god: Gratitude and Blame
Canon 5D- 20mm lens
1/10th f16 50 ISO tripod
Haverton Hill Transporter
Bridge
4th April 2007

Raging Whisper: Deadlines
Canon 5D- 32mm lens
6.2 seconds f14 50 ISO tripod
Yorkshire Dales
26th November 2008

Locked In: The lock
Canon 5D- 168mm lens
1/40th F4 50 ISO tripod
Cragside metal bridge
Northumberland
5th May 2008

Lonely Cloud: Lonely cloud
Canon 5D- 70mm lens
1/20th f8 50 ISO tripod
Haverton Hill
11th April 2007

A-Z: VW
Canon 5D-32mm lens
38 seconds f9 400 ISO tripod
Lyme Regis
26th January 2008

Suntan: The simple things
Canon 5D-24mm lens
1/60th f14 50 ISO tripod
Ice cream advert Suffolk
14th March 2007

Sea: Forever and Never
Canon 5D- 40mm lens
¼ second f11 50 ISO tripod
Whitby North Yorkshire
18th March 2008

White Horses: Sparkle
Canon 5D-200mm lens
0.3 seconds f32 50 ISO
handheld
River Ure Wensleydale
14th June 2008

Grasslands: Grasses
Canon 5D-200mm lens
1/400th f4 50 ISO handheld
The Yorkshire Dales
23rd July 2008

Ashes to Ashes: Pathway
Canon 5D- 65mm lens
0.8 seconds f22 50 ISO
handheld
Shore of Thirlmere Lake
District
Deliberate camera movement
31st October 2007

November Day: Remember
Canon 5D-106mm lens
1/8th f16 400 ISO tripod
Hartlepool war memorial
17th November 2008

**The Troubles:
Broken window**
Canon 5D- 88mm lens
1/8th f14 50 ISO tripod
Shelter Weymouth Dorset
23rd January 2008

Search: Shattered
Canon 5D-200mm lens
1/10th f18 50 ISO tripod
Haverton Hill Teesside
4th November 2007

Anger: After Pollock
Canon 5D-67mm lens
1/200th f4 50 ISO tripod
Graffiti Whitby North
Yorkshire
27th August 2008

**Whether the Weather:
Better days**
Canon G9 43mm lens
1/80th f3.5 100 ISO handheld
Derelict garage in an
otherwise nice part of
Scotland
18th April 2010

**A Poverty Wind: Floating
down the drink**
Canon G9 210mm lens
1/60th f4.8 80 ISO handheld
River Tyne Newcastle
30th June 2009

**30 St Mary Axe:
The Gherkin**
Canon G9 35mm lens
1/50th f5 80 ISO handheld
London
26th August 2009

**The Lost Shoppers: Evening
rush (support image)**
Canon G9 80mm lens
1 second f3.5 80 ISO handheld
Deliberate camera movement
York
12th November 2009

**The Lost Shoppers: The lost
shoppers (main image)**
Casio XP700 24mm lens
1 second f8 handheld 80 ISO
Deliberate camera movement
Middlesbrough
12th January 2006

**Country life: Dancing
rabbits (support image)**
Canon 5D- 50mm lens
0.4 second f8 100 ISO
tripod mounted
Digital painting from
original photograph
30th January 2010

**Country life: Reed beds
(main image)**
Canon 5D- 105mm lens
0.3 seconds f16 50 ISO tripod
Southwold harbour area
Suffolk coast
21st April 2009

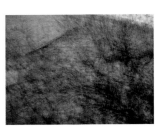

**Seasons: Impression of
a Stone Barn**
Canon 5D 65mm lens
1.3 seconds f16 50 ISO
handheld
Deliberate camera movement
Swaledale North Yorkshire
28th February 2009

**Meadow flowers:
Wildflower meadow**
Mamiya 645 Telephoto
zoom lens
Exposure not recorded
Fuji Velvia (film) 50/32
ISO tripod
Billingham Beck Valley
Summer 1998.

**Winter Trees: Shades of
white (support image)**
Canon 5D- 40mm lens
1.3 seconds f14 100 ISO
tripod
Yorkshire Moors
15th January 2010

**Winter Trees: Littondale
winter (main image)**
Canon 5D- 200mm lens
1/12th f16 50 ISO tripod
Littondale Yorkshire Dales
6th December 2008

**Hunting Baby Rainbows:
Rainbows end**
Canon 5D145mm lens
1/100th f4 50 ISO tripod
Snowdonia
5th September 2007

Waters Edge: Waters Edge
Canon 5D-163mm lens
2.5 seconds f1150 ISO
handheld
Deliberate camera movement
Peat stream Yorkshire Dales
1st February 2007

Buttertubs: Dream of the Dales (support image)
Canon 5D- 200mm lens
1.6 seconds f32 100 ISO
handheld
Deliberate camera movement
Buttertubs Pass the
Yorkshire Dales
14th April 2008

Buttertubs: Buttertubs Pass (main image)
Ebony 54 camera 90mm lens
1 second f22
Fuji Velvia (film) 50/32
ISO tripod
Buttertubs Pass the
Yorkshire Dales
Winter date unknown.

How Big is the Sky?: Big sky over the earth
Canon 5D-105mm lens
1/10th f16 50 ISO tripod
Fields Northumberland
21st February 2009

I am a wave: Wave (support image)
Canon 5D-180mm lens
1 second f6.3 50 ISO handheld
Panning movement on the wave
Whitby North Yorkshire
19th March 2007

I am a wave: Grey sea (main image)
Canon 5D-35mm lens
1/15th f16 50 ISO tripod
The sea Whitby North
Yorkshire
6th June 2008

On the beach 2048: The beach
Ebony 54 camera 90mm lens
Several seconds f22
Fuji Velvia (film) 50/32
ISO tripod
St Bees Head Cumbria
Date not recorded.

Missing You: Gentle tide (support image)
Canon 5D-21mm lens
1 second f20 100 ISO tripod
Dungeness Kent
14th July 2010

Missing You: Lone Gull (main image)
Canon 5D 200mm lens
1/13th f4 50 ISO handheld
Pembrokeshire
20th May 2007

Stockholm Syndrome in the UK: Beach hut days
Casio XP700-35mm lens
1 second f11 80 ISO handheld
Deliberate camera movement
Whitby North Yorkshire
11th May 2006

Leaving : Swaledale barn in a meadow
Pentax 67- 55mm lens
Wide aperture exposure not
recorded tripod
Fuji Velvia
Swaledale near Gunnerside
June.

Flaunt Yourself: The circle game
Canon 5D- 126mm lens
1/15th f6.3 50 ISO tripod
Cut tree Cragside
Northumberland
5th May 2008

Day-trippers : Misty mountains Glencoe
Canon 5D 200mm lens
1 second f14 100 ISO tripod
Glencoe Scotland
17th April 2010

Path: Path
Canon 5D-93mm lens
2.6 seconds f16 50 ISO tripod
Barn in Swaledale
17th Octobre 2008

Transporter Bridge:
Transporter Bridge
Canon 5D-28mm lens
0.3 seconds f16 50 ISO tripod
Middlesbrough
19th February 2008

Angel of the North:
Angel sunset
Canon 5D 35mm lens
4 seconds f16 50 ISO tripod
Gateshead Tyneside
21st February 2009

Steel River: The roar
Canon 5D-200mm lens
1/60th f16 100 ISO tripod
Redcar Steel Works, digital
artwork
13th December 2009

Launch Yourself:
The Great North Run
Canon 5D- 105mm lens
1/5th f22 50 ISO handheld
Deliberate camera movement
Impression of the effort and
texture of the road
5th October 2008

Love Through Time:
Watercolour
Canon 5D- 149mm lens
1.3 seconds f32 100 ISO
handheld
River in Snowdonia
18th September 2009

Saltwick Bay: Shipwreck
Saltwick Bay
Ebony 54 90mm lens
6x12 back
½ second f22 (estimated
not recorded) tripod
Fuji Velvia
North Yorkshire Coast Whitby

Still Standing: Lone tree
limestone and last light
Ebony 54 90mm lens
8 seconds f22 .09ND
Graduated filter tripod
Fuji Velvia
Twislton Scar the Yorkshire
Dales
March 2003

The trip: View of
Swaledale and horse
Fuji 69GXW069111 camera
fixed 65mm lens tripod
Fuji Velvia
Swaledale Yorkshire Dales
Autumn exact date not
known.

A Perfect Moment: Finkle
street Richmond
Ebony 54 camera 240mm lens
6x12 back
1 second f22
Fuji Velvia
Winter.

Togetherness:
Loch Laidon Scotland
Canon 5D- 82mm lens
21 seconds f16 50 ISO tripod
Loch Laidon
4th November 2008

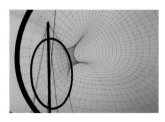

The infant stirs once more:
Temenos
Canon 5D- 126mm lens
1/60th f14 100 ISO tripod
Middlesbrough
30th June 2010